SIMPLE EASY POWERFUL TIPS TO HELP YOU PLAY BETTER GOLF

BOBBY LEWIS

This ebook is optimized for viewing on a computer screen, but it is organized so you can also print it out and assemble it in a binder. Since the text is optimized for screen viewing, the type is larger than that in printed books.

NOTICES

My attorney says I have to include this, so here goes…

This book is designed to provide accurate information on the subject matter covered. While all attempts have been made to verify information provided in this publication, neither the author nor the publisher assumes any responsibility for errors, omissions or contrary interpretation of the subject matter.

This book is sold with the understanding that the publisher and author are not engaged in rendering professional services. If you require the assistance of a professional, you should contact one directly.

The purchaser or reader of this publication assumes responsibility for the use of these materials and information. The author and publisher assume no responsibility or liability whatsoever on behalf of any purchase or reader of these materials.

CONTENTS

INTRODUCTION

There are lots of ways to play golf — some good — some not so good. Two important aspects include a combination of equipment and your mental approach to the game. Yet, nothing is more fundamental than your own personal swing. This is where all of the elements of golf come together and determine your results. It's what separates the novice from advanced players by the formula you use.

Throughout this guide, I'm going to show you some simple… easy… powerful tips that will definitely help improve your golf swing.

CHAPTER 1 :

BASIC FACTORS

Everything in golf is connected. It's as important as pencil and paper to being able to write a letter. So even though my focus is going to be primarily on improving your swing (the pencil), there are some related issues that need to be addressed. This includes your equipment (the paper) and your state of physical fitness (the story in your letter).

CHAPTER 2

CHOOSING THE RIGHT GOLF CLUBS

Although I am going to be more focused on your swing rather than your equipment, it's still important to point out that the golf clubs you're using have a profound effect on your swing.

If a club is too heavy… too light for you… or the wrong length, you won't be able to develop the proper swing. I'm talking about your specific swing, because every golfer's physical abilities and mental capabilities are different.

Whether you're buying or renting your golf clubs, make sure you use ones that are appropriate for your size. You wouldn't wear a size 10 shoe if you fit into a size 12, right? So this logic carries over into the equipment you use, with the same importance.

There are equipment charts available to show you the proper shaft length and correct shaft flex that's right for you, which any golf shop or pro can provide you.

Using the right golf ball is also important. You need to make sure it fits and performs properly to your swing. A golf professional or pro shop can have you swing golf clubs on a swing analyzer to determine your actual swing speed. From this, a club fitter can determine the best shaft flex to fit your swing.

Most golf pro shops and some of the large golf retailers have a club fitter on staff to help you if you need a fitting. Using a custom club fitter is another option, and the one I prefer, simply because they provide more personal service.

Regardless of where you live, custom club fitters/makers are not difficult to find thanks to the world wide web. What's important is quality, experience and the reputation of the club maker. In my case, I've depended on Patriot Golf, a custom club maker located in Owatonna, Minnesota.

Lonny Larson, founder of Patriot Golf, is an experienced club maker who really understands the mechanics of club design. His knowledge and creativity has produced specialty clubs for some of the

RE/MAX Long Driving Champions, who, by the way, have set world records from California to South Africa. In 2011, Lonny earned Golf Digest Magazine's selection as one of the top-qualified club makers in America.

Lonny will work closely with you to get the perfect fit for you. Once you know more about your swing and get fitted to your equipment, then you can choose the golf ball that works best for your game.

LONNY LARSON @ PATRIOT GOLF

Telephone	507-456-1973
Email	patriotgolf@gmail.com
Website	patriotgolf.us

Ball selection may seem trivial, but choosing the right ball really is important.

Let's say you have a 70 to 85 mph swing speed. If you use a high compression ball, you won't have sufficient speed to compress a high compression ball enough to provide you the proper amount of lift as the ball leaves the club. This results in lower ball flights and worm burners that put you out in the weeds.

Just off the top of my head, if your scores are around 85 and up, I recommend using a popular two piece ball such as from Titleist or Bridgestone. They last as long as you can keep finding them off the tee and are pretty much cut resistant.

When your scores get in the high 70's or lower, you can experiment with the more technologically advanced 3 and 4 piece balls. These golf balls perform better for more advanced players with higher swing speeds.

I think you're beginning to see, there's more to choosing just the right clubs and balls, but rather starting with a complete picture of all the right combinations to cover the basics. With practice, you will learn which club combinations bring out your best game. The mental part of the game will complete the whole package.

CHAPTER 3

GETTING FIT FOR GOLF

Although everyone knows golf is a sport, many people downplay the physical aspects of it. Compared to most other sports, golf is slow and doesn't seem to require any great physical exertion. This belief is quite deceptive.

The golf swing actually demands a good amount of physical strength and coordination. Add to this rhythm, tempo and then course management… include a good mental attitude and maintain it for five hours straight… throw in walking up and down steep inclines and hills which can be equivalent to a five mile walk. I've played some tournaments that took 7½ hours to play 18 holes!

The closest analogy to playing golf is probably swinging a bat in baseball, but with golf you need to be much more precise. A baseball slugger, for example, doesn't really care what direction he sends the ball, as long as he hits it. A golfer, on the other hand, must be very precise. He or she needs the power of a slugger and the geometrical precision of a pool shark.

Getting physically fit can help you improve your swing by making you stronger, more agile and more flexible. Flexibility is key and a very important factor. As you'll see later on, you don't want to rely on upper body strength for power when you swing, yet it still helps to be more fit and stronger. Flexibility is the engine to longer, straighter golf shots, starting at the first tee. I've seen so many golfers who haven't adequately prepared themselves in this area.

For this reason, you should not overlook the importance of strength and physical fitness in golf. It's true that players of all sizes and ages can play golf, but you can improve your swing by getting stronger and more coordinated by staying flexible. You'll definitely be more resistant to injuries.

You don't have to be able to run a marathon or bench press 300 pounds, but you should be in the best physical shape possible. If you don't exercise, other than playing golf, you should consider some sort of fitness program. It doesn't have to be anything extreme. It can be something you find enjoyable… or at least tolerable.

Going to the gym two or three times per week is a good option. When you're there, do a combination of weight training (or other type of resistance/strength training) and cardio.

If you prefer to work out in your own home, the treadmill, stair climber or elliptical machine is a good investment.

For weight and strength training you might choose a set of dumbbells or barbells, and power walking to strengthen your cardiovascular system.

NOTE: Always check with your health care provider before starting any exercise program.

When speaking about golf and physical fitness, you can't ignore the importance of core fitness. This refers to the muscles around your mid-section, including the abdominal, back and pelvis. When you swing a golf club, this is where all your power comes from.

You have a variety of exercise and workout options that will strengthen your core…

- Kettlebells

- Medicine Ball (a weighted ball about the size of a basketball)

- Mini trampoline workouts

- Rowing machines

- Abdominal exercises such as crunches, sit-ups and pull-ups

Performing your ab workouts on an exercise ball can make them more challenging. Throwing a medicine ball back and forth is a great way to strengthen your core. Again, consult your physician before starting any exercise program.

Maintaining a level of flexibility is crucial for achieving your best golf swing. It's important to make sure you do some warm-up stretching before and after every workout… this helps you avoid injuries. Yoga or Tia Chi also helps with flexibility.

You don't have to be an elite athlete to develop a good golf swing. It does, however, help you get the most out of your game if you're in good shape. Watch some really talented players… you can learn a lot about improving your golf swing by observing what they do.

No two people have the exact same swing, so you aren't trying to mimic anyone. You can pick up some helpful pointers by watching good players in person, on TV or video.

Most golfers who play the game don't always watch it with a scientific eye. I suggest that instead of watching passively… you closely observe what each player is doing. Pick the players you admire and pay close attention to everything they do. Note everything about their swing… where they look… their hand position… their stance… and how they swing the shaft. This is part of the pre-shot routine… all good players have one and so should you.

It's also helpful to compare the swing of a professional with the swing of a novice and advanced player. By carefully watching good golfers, you're likely to notice a few faults in your own swing that you never noticed before.

CHAPTER 4

VIDEOTAPE YOUR SWING

Here's a great idea… have someone videotape you while you're playing. You can practice your swing in front of a mirror – just don't get too close to the mirror! By having the ability to study your swing, you may notice things that you weren't aware of. You could ask a more advanced player for advice, as well. Another option is to send videos of your golf swing to a golf school that is willing to offer suggestions to help you correct any faults you may have.

I've used Graves Golf Academy in the past and highly recommend their service. You can ask for Todd or Tim Graves at (866) 377-2316. You can send them your video via internet and for a fee in the $95 range, you'll receive a 30-day student lesson, which allows you to send multiple videos to them for analysis. They will review your swing and offer useful tips for improvement. These guys are pros with more than 20 years' experience behind them. They are a trusted resource.

Tell them their former student, crazy Bobby Lewis, sent you. I don't make any profits from this… I just have that much faith in their opinions and believe you'll be satisfied. When you have footage of yourself on tape, it's easy to pinpoint where problems may lie. You can freeze-frame it, slow-mo it, or watch the same swing over and over again to see what you did wrong – or right.

PROPER GOLF GRIP

Before you swing the golf club, you have to grip it. This is the starting point, so let's look at some important tips for gripping the golf club.

- Use moderate strength – you want maximum control but minimum tension in your hands

- Don't hold the club in your palms, but in the middle digits of your fingers

- Make sure your grip is in proper alignment with the club face; always look down before swinging so that the club face will be square with the ball

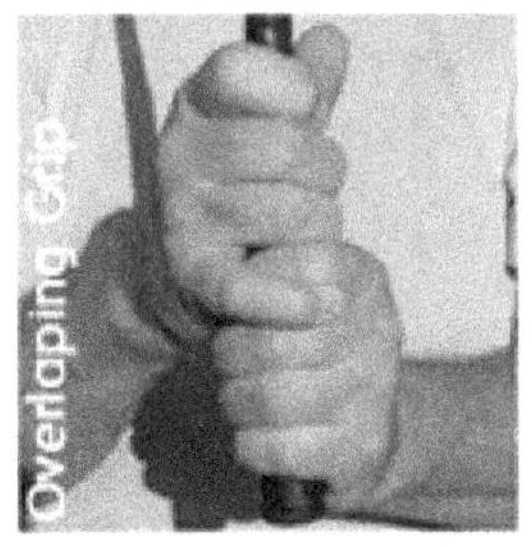

The grip used by most golfers is called the *Overlap Grip*. This is made by taking the pinky of your right hand and placing it over the forefinger of your left hand (if you're left-handed, reverse this).

The *Interlock Grip* is best suited for people with shorter than average fingers. For this grip, you interlock the pinky and index finger instead of having one covering the other.

The third grip that many golfers use is the *10 Finger Grip*. It's called this because all ten fingers are on the golf club, with the pinky of one hand touching the forefinger of the other. This grip is appropriate for weaker players, as it gives you more control and freedom of motion. You can experiment with all three grips until you find the one that suits you best.

CHAPTER 6

YOUR STANCE

Aside from your grip, the other essential factor to consider prior to your swing is your stance. Your stance will depend to some extent on your body type and what makes you comfortable, but there are some general principles to keep in mind.

- ↬ Feet should be approximately shoulder width apart, with knees slightly bent (just enough that they're not locked)

- ↬ Keep your back straight but not tense or rigid – you'll be bending slightly as you swing

When you do bend in preparation for the swing, bend from your hips rather than your shoulders

CHAPTER 7

YOUR GOLF SWING AND THE PIVOT

Let's get down to the nitty-gritty of your golf swing. The first and most important concept to focus on is the pivot. This simply means the pivoting or rotation of your hips as you swing the golf club. This is a simple concept, but many players find it difficult to put into practice.

The first thing to understand is that the pivot is where all of your power comes from. To return to our baseball analogy, it's the same as someone swinging a bat, trying to hit a home run (or even a single). Many golf players think they have to swing harder to make the ball go farther. This isn't the case, and trying to swing too hard will only make you lose control. It can also cause an injury to your lower back!

One of the most common mistakes golfers make is using their arms and shoulders when swinging. Your goal should be to generate all of your power from your hips. This is where the pivot enters the picture.

The pivot is not separate from the swing – it's actually what you should be focusing on as you swing your club. It's the essential motion that determines the successful outcome of your swing.

It's almost impossible to swing a golf club without pivoting, so focus on your hips rather than your hands, arms and shoulders.

CHAPTER 8

YOUR MENTAL STATE AND BREATHING

Your mental state is another important element of your golf swing. Breathing is in the same category because it's something you have to consciously be aware of as part of your golf game. What's more, the way you breathe determines how comfortable and relaxed you are – which, in turn – greatly impacts your swing.

You don't need to go through any elaborate mental exercises before swinging the golf club. Some people recommend visualization, and if you think this helps, by all means do it. It's not essential, yet I think it's a good idea to be swinging to a target. The main thing to keep in mind regarding your mental state is not to let your mind get in the way.

You want to remove as much tension as possible from your mind and body. Obviously, you don't want to be so relaxed that you're daydreaming or not paying attention… what you want is to be relaxed and focused. Your objective is making a good shot. Don't feel like your life depends on it. There's an irony here… caring too much about your shot will end up making it worse, not better!

The main thing to keep in mind about your breathing is to keep doing it! Seriously, when you tense up you tend to hold our breath. Just breathe as naturally as possible as you prepare to take the shot. You will naturally tend to exhale as you swing, but you don't have to memorize any specific breathing routine.

Relaxed breathing is good for your overall health, as well as your golf game. Taking long, deep breaths is the best way to breathe… something that's true at all times, not just when swinging a golf club. You can develop better breathing techniques by taking a yoga class, or from a book or course on the subject.

Proper breathing will help your swing in the long run, because deep breathing helps to generate the kind of power in your hips that you need when pivoting.

So, focus on your breathing to benefit your overall health and fitness, and your golf game.

CHAPTER 9

BREAKING DOWN YOUR SWING

Your goal for the ultimate golf swing is one fluid motion. To best understand how to get there can be broken down into a few parts.

BACKSWING AND DOWNSWING

Developing the best swing has a lot to do with the transition between your backswing and downswing. The backswing is where you bring the golf club back, generating enough momentum to send the ball into the air. This is obviously very important, but it's actually the downswing that gives golfers the most trouble.

The downswing is the part of your swing where your hips and legs guide your hands, arms and shoulders, and the golf club downward. After you complete the backswing, pause for just an instant. Then make a smooth downward motion, generating the power from your hips. Your hands, arms and shoulders should then follow.

FOLLOW-THROUGH

Follow through is a concept that's relevant in many sports. It comes into play when a pool player makes a shot, when a basketball player shoots for the basket or when a boxer throws a punch, just to give a few examples. An athlete's follow through is what creates the throw, shot or punch power and focus.

Follow through is an important part of the golf swing that many golfers have a difficult time with. Not having proper follow through is what causes the dreaded phenomenon in golf known as "the slice". The slice is also known as the banana ball, because the ball follows a curve and slices to the right.

The opposite problem of the slice is the hook shot, where the ball curves to the left. Problems such as hooking or slicing are very common among all golfers, and not just beginners. These shots indicate a basic flaw in the way you're swinging, and this often has to do with lack of follow-through.

You can't just hit the ball… you must swing the shaft back, down and through, with a high finish over your shoulder. If you don't follow through, or finish your swing, you decelerate which causes the ball to hook or slice.

Here are some of the most important things to consider for your follow through:

- Keep your head down and slightly tilted away from your target. Don't make the mistake of raising your head up because that is what changes your swing plane.

- Your right shoulder should remain down, below your left shoulder (opposite for left-handed players).

- As you execute your swing, your weight should shift from the back foot to the front foot during the downswing.

- Your swing should be smooth with no abrupt or jerky motions. You can achieve this by counting "1-2-3" or saying something like "I swing to my target". This creates the proper cadence to help you make a repeatable swing.

You should finish in a balanced position after the swing on your forward foot, with the golf club over your front shoulder and belt buckle, facing your target.

Follow-through is something you'll develop with practice. A lot of it has to do with your mental state. If you're not fully committed to your swing, you will tend to freeze up at some point and not follow through completely. This is why so many beginner and intermediate golfers have a tendency to slice or hook. You're actually hitting at the ball rather than swinging the shaft around your body to the top. This is also known as decelerating.

CHAPTER 10 :

A FLUID SWING

Even though the golf swing can be broken down into elements such as the **backswing, downswing and follow-through**, it should really be one fluid motion. As I've mentioned already, the pivot is an essential part of the swing – the downswing in particular – because that's where all the power is generated, which helps you follow-through to the proper finish.

CHAPTER 11

PRACTICING YOUR GOLF SWING

As with any sport, the more you practice, the better you'll get. It's also important to practice with the right mindset. When you practice, you should be willing to experiment and not worry about the results so much. Pay attention to your stance, grip and technique when practicing, and find out what helps or what makes it worse.

Remember this important point…
when you're experimenting with what works for you, don't swing at more than 60% power. Practice drills can be a very effective way to improve your golf swing.

Once you're hitting balls consistently, you can always increase your power in small increments. Take it easy while you're making changes and increasing speed so you don't swing too hard and lose control. When you're playing golf, you should be concerned about your score, so this is not the time to experiment or make changes. Use your practice time to try new things and see what's effective and works best for you.

If you can't get to the practice range, practice at home in front of a mirror to help you develop better habits. Here are a couple of great tips…

- An excellent exercise to help you determine whether or not you're making a ninety-degree turn in your backswing is to place a piece of blue tape vertically down the center of a full-length mirror and practice turning your forward shoulder past the blue tape.

- As part of this drill, imagine having a big yellow happy face in the center of your back. Visualize that happy face smiling at your target at the top of your backswing. This is the ideal position and indicates that your back is pointing correctly at your target.

The reason to imagine having a sticker in the center of your back is to help you easily make that ninety-degree turn without really thinking about how to do it. All you need to think about is pointing that happy face at your target.

CHAPTER 12

SHOULD YOU TAKE LESSONS

As with any sport, taking lessons from a golf instructor will help you improve your golf game. Instructors aren't hard to find because most practice facilities and golf courses provide a least one golf pro who offers lessons.

The problem with taking lessons is that instructors only teach you the basics, which consist of…

- Grip

- Stance

- Posture

- Swing

What they usually mention only briefly, unless you pay them to go out on the golf course with you, is course management – which is where the real knowledge of the game lies.

For example, some instructors spend most of your lesson time hitting off of a golf range matt. When first learning, the matt is as close to a perfect lie every swing. Then you graduate to the grass when the instructor feels you're ready. But many instructors don't teach you how to use that instruction to transition from the practice range to actually playing on the golf course. So when you're finally out there playing golf, you tend to lose your confidence.

It's certainly necessary to learn the basics, but the real meat in the knowledge of the game comes in course management… this is where the rubber meets the road.

There are so many variables when you're actually out playing and many instructors don't make it a habit of showing you how to play golf out on the course. Anyone can learn to swing a club or hit the ball, but learning good course management is essential. You spend hours learning on the range with your instructor, and then you're off on your own playing the golf course, confused with a loss of confidence.

It's my belief that you should spend equal or more time on course management than what you spend on the driving range. I want to give you some elements of course management I feel are essential to you becoming a better player.

COURSE MANAGEMENT INCLUDES BUT IS NOT LIMITED TO…

- Wind speed and direction

- Temperature and dew point

- Type of grass of the fairways and putting greens

- Thickness and length of different grasses

- Ball position for ball flight

- Club selection for proper distance

- How to hit a ball laying below your feet or above your feet

- How to hit from a downhill lie and an uphill lie

- Speed of greens and direction of break

- Best sections of the green to hit onto

- Which side of the fairway is best to hit from

- What your target shot should be

- What side of the tee box to hit from

- Tee it up or tee it down?

- When to use the knock down shot

Many of these course management lessons and how to use them can be found in my complete golf guide…

38 Tips for Breaking 80:
A-Step-By-Step-Guide-To-Get-You-There

It's always helpful to have someone who is a good player watch your swing and point out some areas where you can improve. Sometimes even a few lessons with a qualified golf pro can work wonders for your game. A golf swing is a subtle thing, and having an expert point out even one minor flaw can make all the difference. This is why I recommended taping your golf swing then using Tim and Todd Graves of Golf Academy earlier in this book.

CHAPTER 13

FINAL THOUGHTS

You can improve your golf swing. It takes a lot of practice and willingness to make changes in the way you normally do things.

Be open to constructive criticism, as long as it's coming from someone who actually knows what they're talking about. Watch good players whenever you can, and try out a few of their techniques to see if they help you.

Most of all… have FUN! You're more likely to make improvements in your golf swing if you're relaxed and enjoying yourself rather than being tense and worried about it.

Golf can greatly enhance your quality of life, especially when you're physically and mentally prepared. Try my suggestions to use clubs that are fitted to you, get physically fit, practice, and videotape yourself while practicing on the range, playing golf out on the course, and even in your own back yard.

For a complete guide and master plan, I recommend picking up my best selling …

<u>38 Tips for Breaking 80:</u>
<u>A Step-By-Step Guide to Get You There</u>.

It takes you step-by-step through every detail you need to know about golfing… in fact, some have called it the "Golfing Manual".

And last but no less important… remember to enjoy yourself… have fun! Golf is game of life for life.

Good luck and happy golfing!

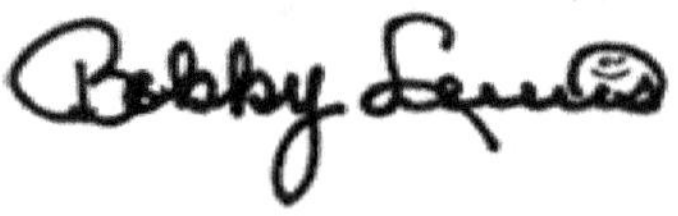

Bobby Lewis
a.k.a. "The Vanilla Gorilla"
Founder, Vanilla Gorilla Golf

A NOTE ABOUT BOBBY

As many of you know, Bobby passed away very suddenly and unexpectedly. The loss of this amazing man will be felt by those who knew and loved him for all time.

Golf was Bobby's passion — he loved nothing more than helping others improve their game and have fun doing it. While he's no longer physically here to teach you, you can still benefit through his books and videos.

The tips contained here in **"Simple Easy Powerful Ways to Help You Improve Your Game"** are a great starting point.

For those of you who would like to completely transform your game, Bobby's best-selling golf guide

<u>"38 Tips for Breaking 80:
A Step-by-Step Guide to Get You There"</u>

will help you do that. It's PACKED with specific pro-level instruction to start you out with awesome accuracy, precision and power. . . and you'll just keep getting better with each game.

Happy Golfing!